Fryderyk

CHOPIN

FIRST DISCOVERY - MUSIC

Written by Catherine Weill
Illustrated by Charlotte Voake
Narrated by Michael Cantwell

The winter was hard in Poland in the year 1810. In spite of the blanket of snow, drums and violins can be heard quite clearly below the windows of a fine red-roofed house near Warsaw: some street musicians have come

LULLABIES OF THE WORLD

All over the world parents sing different lullabies to send their babies to sleep. Yiddish, Irish and Russian lullabies are especially beautiful. Do you remember the tunes your mother or father sang to you?

1 PRELUDE, OP. 28 NO. 1 IN C MAJOR
LULLABY, OP. 57 IN D FLAT MAJOR

to celebrate the birth of a son into the Chopin family. In his cradle little Fryderyk starts to cry with fright. To comfort him his mother hums a sweet, sad song.

Mr Chopin is French and is a French teacher. He wants his son to speak several languages. Soon Fryderyk is learning Latin, Greek and French, and then German, English

and Italian! But the one he likes best of all is the language of music. His mother first introduces him to the piano and, at just five years old, Fryderyk makes up a little tune for his father's birthday.

MUSICAL STORIES

Chopin liked to recount the adventures of his favourite heroes on the piano. His sisters used to try to guess which character each piece was about. They had a lot of fun. You too could try to tell stories by whistling, drumming or using sounds you make with your voice.

Fryderyk was a prodigy at the piano, as if born with the notes already under his fingers. When he was eight he was invited to play for the brother of the Russian Tsar, the Grand Duke, a stern,

FINGERS ON THE KEYS

You can do what you like on the piano! Using the high notes you can imitate a bird, while you can make the low notes sound like a growling wolf... Try telling a story using just one or two fingers on the piano.

10

3 STUDY, OP. 25 NO. 1
IN A FLAT MAJOR

temperamental man. Fryderyk was nervous as he sat down at the piano, but as soon as his fingers touched the keys the palace was full of beautiful sounds. How proud his father was!

As a boy, Fryderyk spent his summer holidays in the country. At one harvest festival the villagers got together and sang to the sound of violins. The peasant girls, all wreathed in flowers, danced and tapped their

4 SONATA FOR CELLO AND PIANO, OP. 65 IN G MINOR, 2ND MOVEMENT, SCHERZO - ALLEGRO CON BRIO

heels. Fryderyk could not resist the rhythm of the music; he grabbed hold of a bass viol and joined in with great enthusiasm.

FESTIVE MUSIC

The rhythms and instruments used give dances their character. Because each country has its own traditions, dances vary from one country to another. Have you ever danced an Irish jig or a tango, the national dance of Argentina?

One evening when he was twelve, Fryderyk's father took him to the opera. Fryderyk was entranced. What joy, drama and passion there was in the mixture of music

5 CONCERTO FOR PIANO AND ORCHESTRA
NO. I, OP. II, IST MOVEMENT, ALLEGRO MAESTOSO

and theatre! How beautifully those voices rose above the orchestra! Later on he would make his piano sing as no-one had ever done before.

PIANO SOUNDS

One day you should open up your piano and see how it works. Did you know that when you press down a key, a little hammer strikes a string, producing a sound? When Chopin's music makes the piano sing you easily forget how the instrument works!

One day, as he was coming out of church, his eyes met those of a young girl of his own age. Fryderyk fell hopelessly in love. Her name was Constance and she had a

SINGING WITH FEELING

Try taking a song that you know really well and changing it by expressing through it something you feel strongly: slow it down; sing it louder and louder; put a stress on certain consonants... See if your friends can guess what feelings you are trying to express.

beautiful voice and dreamt of becoming a singer. But Fryderyk was too shy to express his love, except through the piano, his trusted friend.

By the time he was seventeen Fryderyk Chopin had already played in many concerts. He was by now a famous pianist and admired as a composer in Poland. But he wanted the world to hear his music. At the age of twenty

18

A UNIVERSAL LANGUAGE

Have you noticed that a lot of music we like listening to comes from different parts of the world? Have you ever thought that somewhere on the other side of the world someone of your own age listens and dances to the same music as you?

7 SONATA NO. 2, OP. 35, 1ST MOVEMENT, GRAVE – DOPPIO MOVIMENTO

he decided he must leave Poland!
As the coach took him off on his
travels, his heart ached at
the thought of those he
was leaving behind…

19

Fryderyk moved to Paris. In the studio of the painter Eugene Delacroix he met George Sand, a famous woman writer. They fell passionately in love. The great musician was now the master of his art. He was a success whenever he played and Paris showered him with praise.

PARIS ARTISTIC CENTRE

In Paris Chopin met other musicians like Franz Liszt, writers like Victor Hugo, and painters... These artists all expressed their feelings very freely in their work and so came to be known as the 'romantics'.

8 FANTASY-IMPROMPTU, OP. 66

Today

as in the past

Chopin's

music

is played

and loved.

THE STUDIES

Chopin had no more piano lessons after the age of twelve. But he devoted himself to this instrument throughout his whole life. This is very unusual in the history of music. As soon as he came to Paris, Chopin began to give lessons. Pianists from all over Europe became his pupils and he dedicated many of his compositions to them. He was a brilliant pianist and a genius at improvisation. His studies are extremely difficult to play and are terrifying tests of skill. But they greatly widened the range of sound that can be produced on the piano.
By composing his twenty-four studies, Chopin truly helped create the modern piano.

Chopin probably began his piano playing on a forte-piano, which has quiet, muffled tones. Later pianos made by Pleyel provided Chopin with a very different instrument.

The difficulty of Chopin's music encouraged piano makers to improve their instruments. This piano by Pleyel, said to belong to Chopin, is very different from earlier models.

9 STUDY, OP. 25 NO. 10
IN B MINOR

THE MAZURKAS

In 1830 Chopin left Poland; he did not return. But he never forgot the dance tunes his mother played on the piano, nor the songs and dances of the village festivals. So through music he was able to recall his native country. He wrote polonaises – noble, heroic dances. He also composed elegant, refined waltzes and more than fifty mazurkas. These mazurkas are Chopin's particular speciality. In a three-time dance rhythm, they reflect his longing and his changeable moods. Some are despairing, others are joyful; some are both. The one you are about to hear combines sadness and joy.

Dancing is still very much a tradition in Eastern Europe. On the opposite page you can see polka dancers in Polish national dress. Below you can see waltzing couples at the annual ball in the Vienna Opera House.

Many ballet pupils do their exercises to the sound of Chopin's waltzes.

10 POLONAISE, OP. 53
MAZURKA, OP. 67 NO. 3 IN C MAJOR

NOCTURNES AND BALLADES

Chopin's music reflects his dreams. The piano is his mirror: all his sensitivity and his feelings are expressed through it. In George Sand's beautiful house in Nohant Chopin adored the romantic atmosphere at dusk and felt in harmony with the secret whisperings as daylight faded. It was there that he composed his ballades and nocturnes. A ballade is like a poem for an instrument that tells a story. Nocturnes are reveries – dreamy pieces – or musical love letters. Chopin used to say 'If you want to play the piano, you have to make it sing'. In the following nocturne listen to how the music sings and breathes just like a human voice. You can recognize Chopin's music by this voice-like quality.

Memories of Chopin are still very much alive at Nohant, George Sand's house in the Indre region of France. Music festivals are held there every year. One of the composer's pianos is still in the drawing room.

It was in Chopin's time that pianists first played on their own at public concerts. This is what we now call a piano recital.

11 **BALLADE NO. 1, OP. 23 IN G MINOR**
NOCTURNE, OP. 27 NO. 1 IN C SHARP MINOR

JOHANN SEBASTIAN BACH
LUDWIG VAN BEETHOVEN
HECTOR BERLIOZ
FRYDERYK CHOPIN
CLAUDE DEBUSSY
GEORGE FRIDERIC HANDEL
WOLFGANG AMADEUS MOZART
HENRY PURCELL
FRANZ SCHUBERT
ANTONIO VIVALDI